FROM A
FATHER'S
Heart
TO A
SON

FROM A
FATHER'S
Heart
TO A
SON

DAVID SHIBLEY

New Leaf Press

First Printing
October 1995

ISBN: 0-89221-309-4
Library of Congress Catalog: 95-71121

DEDICATION
To my sons,
Jonathan and Joel,
the inspiration for this book
and a constant inspiration
to their parents.

*One generation shall praise Your works to
another, and shall declare Your mighty
acts (Ps. 145:4).*

Introduction

A few years ago, a friend paid me a compliment. "David," he said, "you're raising two really good boys." Of course, I was humbled, grateful, and painfully aware of my shortcomings as a dad. But since we're good friends I also felt I could make an important adjustment to what he said.

"Jim," I replied, "you've encouraged me today. But my intent has never been to raise good boys. I want to raise good *men*."

For fathers of sons, that really is the point, isn't it? God entrusts us, families expect us, the Church compels us, society pleads with us — *"Give us good and godly men."* For those commissioned with the precious gift of sons, this is our calling, privilege, and challenge.

The apostle Paul issued a sacred charge when he said, "Fathers, do not provoke your children to wrath, but bring them up in the training and admonition of the Lord" (Eph. 6:4). You can use this book as a tool in that process, helping turn good boys into men of integrity. I pray it will find its way into the hands of sons at Christmas, on birthdays, and at graduations, as a gift from fathers to sons. I also pray that it will be pulled out of soggy pockets on fishing trips, out of desks during spare minutes, and out of car pockets on the way to and from ballgames.

The test laboratory for these principles has been our family. My sons bear witness that these principles, while cherished, are fleshed out imperfectly at best by me.

My collaborator in this grand experiment of transforming good boys into godly men has been Naomi, my college sweetheart, my wife of almost a quarter century, and the wonderful mother of our sons. Early test results (our sons are in their late teens and early twenties) indicate very gratifying outcomes as these principles have been applied. The success I have seen in our sons is due to the veracity of the principles and the beauty of their mother's character. She has consistently expemplified the truths this book shares.

Yet, in another respect, the success of raising godly young men can be attributed only marginally to either of us as parents. We thank God for the decisions our sons themselves have made. For all of us, the quality of our lives is determined by our choices. Naomi and I are grateful to have lived with two level-headed, disciplined, and God-honoring young men. I've learned many valuable lessons from them.

Since before our sons were born, their lives have been dedicated to Jesus Christ and His purposes. That is why, as we used to tuck them into bed at night, our "lullaby" was a song about life's purpose. We wanted these to be the last words our sons heard before they drifted to sleep. We believed that as they slept God's

Spirit would knead this challenge into their young hearts. It is the same challenge I now leave with you:

Rise up, O men of God,
Have done with lesser things,
Give heart and soul and mind and strength
To serve the King of kings.
Rise up, O men of God,
The church for you does wait.
Her strength unequal to her task,
Rise up, and make her great!

From a father's heart,
David Shibley

Sections

YOUR PERSONAL DEVELOPMENT
YOUR RELATIONSHIPS
YOUR MARRIAGE AND FAMILY
YOUR FINANCES
YOUR LIFE'S WORK AND CONTRIBUTION

YOUR
PERSONAL
DEVELOPMENT

It is more important what God does *in* you than what He does *through* you, because the quality of what He does through you will be determined by the quality of what He does in you. God will allow things to happen *to* you so that things can happen *in* you so that things can happen *through* you.

Being confident of this very thing, that He who has begun a good work in you will complete it until the day of Jesus Christ (Phil. 1:6).

**Always honor the person
and work of the Holy Spirit.**

*And do not grieve the Holy Spirit of God,
by whom you were sealed for the day of
redemption (Eph. 4:30).*

*Do not quench the Spirit
(1 Thess. 5:19).*

As a Christian, your core values are faith, hope, and love. So fight any tendency to be a skeptic, a cynic, or a critic. It eats away at the essence of who you are as a believer in Christ.

And now abide faith, hope, love, these three; but the greatest of these is love (1 Cor. 13:13).

Salvation is an absolutely free gift through faith in Christ. But this does not mean you have no further accountability to God. Now, in Christ, you are truly free to be all you can be. You are not saved by good works, but you are saved *to* good works and these are produced by Christ's life in you.

For by grace you have been saved through faith, and that not of yourselves; it is the gift of God, not of works, lest anyone should boast. For we are His workmanship, created in Christ Jesus for good works, which God prepared beforehand that we should walk in them (Eph. 2:8-10).

**Your two most important days are
today and *that day* — that day when
you will stand before Jesus Christ and
give an account of your life. Live today
in light of that day.**

*For we must all appear before the
judgment seat of Christ, that each one may
receive the things done in the body
according to what he has done, whether
good or bad* (2 Cor. 5:10).

Generally speaking, your physical well-being after 40 will be in direct proportion to the care you have given to your body before then. Develop a lifestyle of consistent, moderate exercise and a God-honoring intake of food.

Or do you not know that your body is the temple of the Holy Spirit who is in you, whom you have from God, and you are not your own? For you were bought at a price; therefore glorify God in your body and in your spirit, which are God's (1 Cor. 6:19-20).

Make a daily time with God priority number one. Few habits could provide more of an anchor for your life than a daily time of praise, prayer, and meditation in God's Word.

O God, You are my God; early will I seek You; my soul thirsts for You; my flesh longs for You (Ps. 63:1).

Always put Jesus first — first in your time, first in your treasure, and most of all, first in your heart.

You shall have no other gods before Me (Exod. 20:3).

My son, give me your heart, and let your eyes observe my ways (Prov. 23:26).

You live in a time when you will have ample opportunities to compromise morally. Make a choice now against "secret" sins of the flesh. Remember, there is no such thing as a "victim-less" sin. Even so-called private sins are victimizing because they limit your potential and grieve the Holy Spirit.

I will set nothing wicked before my eyes (Ps. 101:3).

Make a formal presentation of your body to God. This should be a definite experience, just as real as your salvation. Voluntarily present yourself to God for His service.

I beseech you therefore, brethren, by the mercies of God, that you present your bodies a living sacrifice, holy, acceptable to God, which is your reasonable service. And do not be conformed to this world, but be transformed by the renewing of your mind, that you may prove what is that good and acceptable and perfect will of God (Rom. 12:1-2).

The only way to live a life that is pleasing to God is by being filled with the Holy Spirit and yielding to His control.

And do not be drunk with wine, in which is dissipation; but be filled with the Spirit (Eph. 5:18).

**Aggressively pursue God's
favor on your life.**

*We are fools for Christ's sake, but you are
wise in Christ! We are weak, but you are
strong! You are distinguished, but we are
dishonored!* (1 Cor. 4:10).

In your lifetime, it may prove very costly to be a committed Christian. Persecution may come. But whatever comes, *always* be loyal to Jesus Christ. The time to settle the loyalty issue isn't when the test comes, it's now.

For if we live, we live to the Lord; and if we die, we die to the Lord. Therefore, whether we live or die, we are the Lord's (Rom. 14:8).

The quickest way to a clean life is by reverencing God and His Word.

How can a young man cleanse his way? By taking heed according to Your word. With my whole heart I have sought You; oh, let me not wander from Your commandments! Your word I have hidden in my heart, that I might not sin against You (Ps. 119:9–11).

No sin is more powerful than God's grace; no transgression is more potent than Jesus' blood.

"Come now, and let us reason together," says the Lord, "though your sins are like scarlet, they shall be as white as snow; though they are red like crimson, they shall be as wool" (Isa. 1:18).

Your acceptance before God is not based on what you have done but rather on what Jesus did for you on the Cross. Never get over the wonder of God's grace or the glory of Christ's sacrifice.

But God forbid that I should boast except in the cross of our Lord Jesus Christ, by whom the world has been crucified to me, and I to the world (Gal. 6:14).

Don't take yourself too seriously. Learn to relax. Learn to laugh. Don't become "a legend in your own mind."

He brought out His people with joy, His chosen ones with gladness (Ps. 105:43).

Dawson Trotman, founder of the Navigators, practiced a nightly discipline he called "HWLW — His Word the last word." As you drift to sleep at night, meditate on God and His Word.

Blessed is the man who walks not in the counsel of the ungodly, nor stands in the path of sinners, nor sits in the seat of the scornful; but his delight is in the law of the Lord, and in His law he meditates day and night (Ps. 1:1-2).

At the beginning of each day, present the day and its activities to God. At the close of each day, do the same.

From the rising of the sun to its going down the Lord's name is to be praised (Ps. 113:3).

He who always speaks the truth doesn't have to worry about covering his tracks!

Therefore, putting away lying, "Let each one of you speak truth with his neighbor" (Eph. 4:25).

Don't rely on your own abilities. Rather, yield yourself, moment by moment, to the control of the Holy Spirit.

Walk in the Spirit, and you shall not fulfill the lust of the flesh (Gal. 5:16).

God is scanning the planet looking for perfect-hearted men. When He finds them, He will bend over backward to honor them. You may never be a perfect man, but you *can* serve God with a perfect heart.

For the eyes of the Lord run to and fro throughout the whole earth, to show Himself strong on behalf of those whose heart is loyal to Him (2 Chron. 16:9).

The most embarrassing times of my life have been when I have been called into question for something foolish that I said. Think before you speak!

Let the words of my mouth and the meditation of my heart be acceptable in Your sight, O Lord, my strength and my Redeemer (Ps. 19:14).

Within your lifetime you will have the opportunity to taste both success and defeat, need and affluence. Be sure to learn the proper lessons in each situation. In success, learn humility. In defeat, learn hope. In need, learn faith. In affluence, learn generosity.

I have learned in whatever state I am, to be content: I know how to be abased, and I know how to abound. Everywhere and in all things I have learned both to be full and to be hungry, both to abound and to suffer need. I can do all things through Christ who strengthens me (Phil. 4:11-13).

Watch out for the subtle tendencies toward idolatry in our culture. Your heart can idolize glamorous people, sports personalities, even inanimate things like cars! Never put anything else on the throne of your heart that belongs to God and God alone.

Little children, keep yourselves from idols (1 John 5:21).

Watch your mouth! There are more ways to take God's name in vain than by cursing. Exercise both reverence and faith when you refer to the Father, the Son, and the Holy Spirit.

That at the name of Jesus every knee should bow, of those in heaven, and of those on earth, and of those under the earth, and that every tongue should confess that Jesus Christ is Lord, to the glory of God the Father (Phil. 2:10-11).

God has placed the Sabbath principle
in the universe. Although we are under
the New Covenant, the principle
still holds true: Work six days.
Sanctify the seventh unto the Lord.

*There remains therefore a rest for the
people of God* (Heb. 4:9).

Here are two sides of the same coin: Always have the courage to risk. Never attempt any new venture without the peace of God in your hearts.

And let the peace of God rule in your hearts (Col. 3:15).

God put this immutable principle
in the universe: Humble yourself before
Him and He will exalt you.

*"God resists the proud, but gives grace to
the humble." Therefore humble yourselves
under the mighty hand of God, that He
may exalt you in due time* (1 Pet. 5:5-6).

Before making any major decision, seek godly counsel.

Where there is no counsel, the people fall; but in the multitude of counselors there is safety (Prov. 11:14).

There is a time to make vows to God.
But let your vows be sacred and rare.
Always be careful to fulfill
any vow you make to God.

*When you make a vow to God, do not delay
to pay it; for He has no pleasure in fools.
Pay what you have vowed — better not to
vow than to vow and not pay*
(Eccles. 5:4-5).

When you come before the Lord,
never claim any merit of your own.
"Nothing in my hands I bring,
simply to the cross I cling."

Blessed are the poor in spirit, for theirs is the kingdom of heaven (Matt. 5:3).

**True meekness is by no means weakness.
Meekness is strength under control.
Those who can control their strength
have awesome authority.**

*He who is slow to anger is better than the
mighty, and he who rules his spirit than he
who takes a city* (Prov. 16:32).

The greatest asset you can possess is motivation. Ask the Holy Spirit for the blessing of spiritual hunger and thirst.

The desire of the righteous will be granted (Prov. 10:24).

Learn to put a proper value on things money cannot buy. The value of the dollar will fluctuate throughout your life, but the value of a good reputation will only increase year by year.

A good name is to be chosen rather than great riches, loving favor rather than silver and gold (Prov. 22:1).

It takes years to build a reputation
of godly character. It takes only
one poor decision to wreck it.

*Keep your heart with all diligence. For out
of it spring the issues of life* (Prov. 4:23).

I have noticed throughout my life that God doesn't respond to my fears; He responds to my faith. Faith gets God's attention. When God speaks, let your heart say "yes" and let your feet obey.

But without faith it is impossible to please Him, for he who comes to God must believe that He is, and that He is a rewarder of those who diligently seek Him (Heb. 11:6).

Never question the absolute authority of Scripture. Doubt your doubts, but trust the Word of God.

My son, give attention to my words; incline your ear to my sayings. Do not let them depart from your eyes; keep them in the midst of your heart; for they are life to those who find them, and health to all their flesh (Prov. 4:20-22).

The things that wreck men's lives are just multiple variations on a few sordid themes: the abuse of money, the abuse of sex, the abuse of power, the abuse of alcohol and drugs, poor time management, and the adopting of an embittered attitude.

What, my son? And what, son of my womb? And what, son of my vows? Do not give your strength to women, nor your ways to that which destroys kings (Prov. 31:2-3).

YOUR
RELATIONSHIPS

**A good thing to remember
And a better thing to do
Is to work with the construction gang
And not with the wrecking crew.**

*Therefore let us pursue the things which
make for peace and the things by which
one may edify another* (Rom. 14:19).

Choose your fights carefully. Only contend for that which is truly non-negotiable and even then, do so in a gracious, non-vindictive spirit. Otherwise, be a peacemaker.

Blessed are the peacemakers, for they shall be called sons of God (Matt. 5:9).

Get enough education so that no
one can ever look down on you. Then
get enough education so you will never
look down on anyone else.

*Be kindly affectionate to one another with
brotherly love, in honor giving preference
to one another* (Rom. 12:10).

Count on it: Someone (probably someone close to you) is going to hurt you. Learn to be a quick, full forgiver. *Never* allow hurt to grow inward and make you bitter. Bitterness is cancerous to the spirit.

Pursue peace with all people, and holiness, without which no one will see the Lord: looking carefully lest anyone fall short of the grace of God; lest any root of bitterness springing up cause trouble, and by this many become defiled (Heb. 12:14-15).

**When wronged by another person, go out
of your way to affirm and honor him
when his name comes up in conversation.**

*See that no one renders evil for evil to
anyone, but always pursue what is good
both for yourselves and for all*
(1 Thess. 5:15).

Get in an accountability group with other Christian men who will hold your feet to the fire in matters of morality, business ethics, and family responsibilities.

As iron sharpens iron, so a man sharpens the countenance of his friend (Prov. 27:17).

You are the only person on planet Earth who can throw you out of God's will for your life. No one's words against you, no one's actions against you can throw you out of God's will for your life. No one has that kind of authority over you; only you have the power to do that.

But none of these things move me; nor do I count my life dear to myself, so that I may finish my race with joy, and the ministry which I have received from the Lord Jesus, to testify to the gospel of the grace of God (Acts 20:24).

Some men make a game of cutting corners — whether it's in paying their taxes, seeing how much they can flirt and still be considered moral, or always trying to redefine the limits of the law. Don't be part of that crowd.

See then that you walk circumspectly, not as fools but as wise, redeeming the time, because the days are evil (Eph. 5:15).

Unfortunately, you live in a time when too many men have a low regard for women. Always show proper respect and esteem toward women. Jesus had no problem calling some men a bunch of snakes but he never spoke a harsh word to a woman.

Do not rebuke an older man, but exhort him as a father, younger men as brothers, older women as mothers, younger women as sisters, with all purity (1 Tim. 5:1-2).

Never despise the poor in your
heart. Always look for ways to
relieve their suffering and lift
them out of their poverty.

*He who mocks the poor reproaches his
Maker; he who is glad at calamity will not
go unpunished (Prov. 17:5).*

Give special care and consideration to children and to the elderly. If you care for them, God will care for you.

Now we exhort you, brethren, warn those who are unruly, comfort the fainthearted, uphold the weak, be patient with all (1 Thess. 5:14).

You need three men in your life: a Paul, a Timothy, and a Barnabas. Find a mentor, find someone to mentor, and find someone to encourage you.

You therefore, my son, be strong in the grace that is in Christ Jesus. And the things that you have heard from me among many witnesses, commit these to faithful men who will be able to teach others also (2 Tim. 2:1-2).

**Always exalt Jesus in your speech.
Be quick to share your faith with
both courage and courtesy.**

*But sanctify the Lord God in your hearts,
and always be ready to give a defense to
everyone who asks you a reason for the
hope that is in you, with meekness and fear*
(1 Pet. 3:15).

**When it comes to judging sin,
be ruthless on yourself and full of
grace toward others.**

*The merciful man does good for his
own soul, but he who is cruel troubles
his own flesh (Prov. 11:17).*

**Cherish every friendship.
Never throw a friend away.**

*Do not forsake your own friend or your
father's friend* (Prov. 27:10).

The finest hour in any relationship is when you have the privilege of standing by a friend who is under attack.

A friend loves at all times, and a brother is born for adversity (Prov. 17:17).

No sexual experience outside of marriage could possibly be worth what it would cost you.

Keep my soul, and deliver me; let me not be ashamed, for I put my trust in You. Let integrity and uprightness preserve me, for I wait for You (Ps. 25:20-21).

A person's worth is not based primarily on his or her potential. There is dignity and great worth in every person because people are made in the image of God. People are also of enormous value because of the price that was paid for their redemption.

Knowing that you were not redeemed with corruptible things, like silver or gold . . . but with the precious blood of Christ, as of a lamb without blemish and without spot (1 Pet. 1:18-19).

In all probability, God has not called you to publicly denounce the shortcomings of others, especially His ministers. Your God is so powerful He is able to correct His servants without any help from you!

For there is nothing covered that will not be revealed, and hidden that will not be known (Matt. 10:26).

Take the word "hate" out of your vocabulary. Character assassination is as surely an act of brutality as physical assassination.

Bless those who persecute you; bless and do not curse (Rom. 12:14).

If you look for ways to lift others,
you will naturally climb pretty
high on the ladder yourself.
Like Jesus, be a servant-leader.

He who is greatest among you, let him be
as the younger, and he who governs as he
who serves (Luke 22:26).

In our culture, there are many sophisticated ways to steal — from the desecrating of another's property to the stealing of information or applause. Make sure that you're a partaker of none of the above.

Let him who stole steal no longer, but rather let him labor, working with his hands what is good, that he may have something to give him who has need (Eph. 4:28).

Don't desire anything God has given to someone else. What God gave as a blessing to another, if coveted and then taken wrongfully, would become a curse to you.

Take heed and beware of covetousness, for one's life does not consist in the abundance of the things he possesses (Luke 12:15).

Media's bombardment of our emotions has tended to desensitize us to human need. Don't lose the valuable asset of empathy.

Rejoice with those who rejoice, and weep with those who weep (Rom. 12:15).

Be a reconciler. Commit to building quality relationships with men of other ethnic backgrounds, other denominations, and even other basic beliefs. Only Christ can reconcile men to God, but He has entrusted us with the job of reconciling men to one another.

Now all things are of God, who has reconciled us to Himself through Jesus Christ, and has given us the ministry of reconciliation, that is, that God was in Christ reconciling the world to Himself, not imputing their trespasses to them, and has committed to us the word of reconciliation. Now then, we are ambassadors for Christ (2 Cor. 5:18-20).

YOUR
MARRIAGE
AND
FAMILY

Learn the value of recreation. Take mini-vacations. When you're single, take them alone. When you're married, with your family. And be sure to block out an annual get-away time with your family. A family vacation will be one of your best investments.

Come to Me, all you who labor and are heavy laden, and I will give you rest. Take My yoke upon you and learn from Me, for I am gentle and lowly in heart, and you will find rest for your souls. For My yoke is easy and My burden is light (Matt. 11:28-30).

Honor the Lord by purposing in your heart now that your only sexual relationship will be with your wife. Keep yourself pure as a gift both to God and to your wife.

For this is the will of God, your sanctification: that you should abstain from sexual immorality; that each of you should know how to possess his own vessel in sanctification and honor, not in passion of lust, like the Gentiles who do not know God (1 Thess. 4:3-5).

If God gives you the wonderful gift of children, don't let a day go by without pronouncing God's blessing over their lives. This is a spiritual right and responsibility of fathers.

The Lord bless you and keep you; the Lord make His face shine upon you, and be gracious to you; the Lord lift up His countenance upon you, and give you peace (Num. 6:24-26).

**A good marriage is made up of
two great forgivers. Be slow to anger
and quick to forgive.**

*And be kind to one another, tenderhearted,
forgiving one another, even as God in
Christ forgave you* (Eph. 4:32).

**When you get married, don't stop dating!
Take your wife out every week.**

Rejoice with the wife of your youth
(Prov. 5:18).

People crave affirmation. Develop the practice of frequent, honest appreciation and affirmation, starting with your wife and children.

Let no corrupt word proceed out of your mouth, but what is good for necessary edification, that it may impart grace to the hearers (Eph. 4:29).

Always compliment your wife — to her face and behind her back!

Husbands, likewise, dwell with them with understanding, giving honor to the wife, as the weaker vessel, and as being heirs together of the grace of life, that your prayers may not be hindered (1 Pet. 3:7).

The only limits on what your children can become are the verbal boundaries you speak over them. Tell them all they can be as they yield their lives to God.

And you fathers, do not provoke your children to wrath, but bring them up in the training and admonition of the Lord (Eph. 6:4).

**Other than Jesus, your wife should always
be your dearest friend.**

*He who finds a wife finds a good thing, and
obtains favor from the Lord (Prov. 18:22).*

**Adultery is not first an act of your body.
Unfaithfulness always begins
as an affair of the heart.**

*You have heard that it was said to those of
old, "You shall not commit adultery." But I
say to you that whoever looks at a woman
to lust for her has already committed
adultery with her in his heart*
(Matt. 5:27-28).

**Respect for parents includes an
appreciation of your heritage, an
acknowledging of all that has made
you what you are — a unique family
background mixed with
both triumph and tragedy.**

*"Honor your father and mother," which is
the first commandment with promise: "that
it may be well with you and you may live
long on the earth* (Eph. 6:2).

YOUR
FINANCES

Never risk your core capital. Take
studied risks with money you could afford
to lose in a worst case scenario.
Otherwise, invest conservatively.

*According to the grace of God which was
given to me, as a wise master builder I
have laid the foundation, and another
builds on it. But let each one take heed how
he builds on it* (1 Cor. 3:10).

John Wesley gave some financial
advice I'll pass along to you. "Give
10 per cent, save 10 per cent and spend
the rest with thanksgiving." I would only
add that your percentage of giving to
God's work and other worthy causes
should increase year by year.

*"Bring all the tithes into the storehouse,
that there may be food in My house, and
try Me now in this," says the Lord of hosts,
"if I will not open for you the windows of
heaven and pour out for you such a
blessing that there will not be room enough
to receive it"* (Mal. 3:10).

**Ten percent of your income belongs
to God's work through your church.
Beyond that, listen for God's directive
in your giving. Then give in faith,
believing God to multiply both your
gift and your ability to give.**

*And God is able to make all grace abound
toward you, that you, always having all
sufficiency in all things, may have an
abundance for every good work. As it is
written: "He has dispersed abroad, he has
given to the poor; his righteousness
endures forever"* (2 Cor. 9:8-9).

Start a consistent savings program *immediately!* Whenever you receive a paycheck, pay God first and then pay yourself. Give your first 10 percent to God and your next 10 percent to yourself and your family in secure savings.

My son, be wise, and make my heart glad (Prov. 27:11).

Credit is easy to get but debt is hard to get out of. If you must acquire debt, make sure it is manageable and short-term. Don't let credit cards proliferate and never max them out.

Owe no one anything except to love one another (Rom. 13:8).

**Be extravagant in your faith
and lavish in what you sow in
secret into God's work.**

*Give, and it will be given to you: good
measure, pressed down, shaken together,
and running over will be put into your
bosom. For with the same measure that
you use, it will be measured back to you
(Luke 6:38).*

Always pay bills on time. If you
want a good name, don't ever believe
that a bill is due "in 90 days." A bill
is due when you receive it.

Render therefore to all their due: taxes to
whom taxes are due, customs to whom
customs, fear to whom fear, honor to whom
honor (Rom. 13:7).

Don't co-sign a note for a friend —
or anyone else. Although it may seem
you are doing him a favor, it is a long-
term risk both to the money involved
and to your friendship.

*My son, if you become surety for your
friend, if you have shaken hands in pledge
for a stranger, you are snared by the words
of your mouth; you are taken by the words
of your mouth* (Prov. 6:1-2).

You will never become wealthy merely on the salary you make. Real wealth is the result of wise investing.

Riches and honor are with me, enduring riches and righteousness (Prov. 8:18).

Before making any investment, become fully informed. Read, research, pray, and listen to seasoned counsel. Equipped with that knowledge, if your heart is still at peace, invest in faith, trusting God for excellent returns.

Plans are established by counsel; by wise counsel wage war (Prov. 20:18).

**Leave a financial inheritance,
not only for your children but also
for your grandchildren.**

*A good man leaves an inheritance to his
children's children* (Prov. 13:22).

YOUR
LIFE'S
WORK
AND
CONTRIBUTION

Make a study of spiritual gifts. Assess your natural abilities and discover your spiritual gifts. You will be most fulfilled in your vocation when your job is a good match for both your natural talents and spiritual gifts.

For I say, through the grace given to me, to everyone who is among you, not to think of himself more highly than he ought to think, but to think soberly, as God has dealt to each one a measure of faith. . . . Having then gifts differing according to the grace that is given to us, let us use them (Rom. 12:3,6).

It is good to pray, "Lord, what is Your will for my life?" But it's even better to pray, "Lord, what is Your will for my *generation* and how do You want my life to fit into Your plan for my times?"

For You are my rock and my fortress; therefore, for Your name's sake, lead me and guide me (Ps. 31:3).

Exercise the gifts God has given you and pursue His best gifts.

There are diversities of gifts, but the same Spirit. There are differences of ministries, but the same Lord. And there are diversities of activities, but it is the same God who works all in all. But the manifestation of the Spirit is given to each one for the profit of all. . . . But earnestly desire the best gifts (1 Cor. 12:4-7,31).

Get global in your thinking. Identify with the body of Christ around the world. Stretch the borders of your intercession.

Do you not say, "There are still four months and then comes the harvest"? Behold, I say to you, lift up your eyes and look at the fields, for they are already white for harvest! (John 4:35).

Measure your success in light of this question: What am I doing to influence the *next* generation for Jesus Christ?

We will not hide them from their children, telling to the generation to come the praises of the Lord, and His strength and His wonderful works that He has done (Ps. 78:4).

One ship goes east, the other west
By the self-same winds that blow.
'Tis the set of the sail and not the gale
That determines the way they go.

Like the ships at sea are the ways of man
As we voyage along through life.
'Tis the set of the soul that decides the goal
And not the calm or strife.
— Ella Wheeler Wilcox

If then you were raised with Christ, seek those things which are above, where Christ is, sitting at the right hand of God. Set your mind on things above, not on things on the earth (Col. 3:1-2).

There is no short cut to lasting success. Anything of real value will require hard, long work. There is exhilaration in work toward a worthy goal, but it's work, none the less. As Bob Pierce said, "The secret to lasting success is *lasting*."

My eyes shall be on the faithful of the land (Ps. 101:6).

Stand for the right and stand with the righteous even if — *especially if* — it costs you something. There is a pay-off.

Blessed are those who are persecuted for righteousness' sake, for theirs is the kingdom of heaven (Matt. 5:10).

Be mature enough to understand that a full compensation for a godly life will take another world. Pursue ultimate success. Ultimate success has little if anything to do with what side of town you live on or what make of car you drive. It has everything to do with whether you hear Jesus pronounce His "well done" over your life.

Well done, good and faithful servant; you were faithful over a few things. I will make you ruler over many things. Enter into the joy of your lord (Matt. 25:21).

My friend from Sri Lanka, Colton Wicknamaratne, has rightly observed that "God's method is a man." Be available for God's purposes. Lay down your agenda for His.

Also I heard the voice of the Lord, saying, "Whom shall I send, and who will go for Us?" Then I said, "Here am I! Send me" (Isa. 6:8).

Be a "gap man." By your godly
life and by your intercession, give
God a reason to avert judgment
and bring revival instead.

*So I sought for a man among them who
would make a wall, and stand in the gap
before Me on behalf of the land, that I
should not destroy it; but I found no one*
(Ezek. 22:30).

God did not place your life at the gateway to a new millennium by chance. You are here at this pivotal point in history to provide a new generation of godly leadership. Discover and pursue your destiny.

Yet who knows whether you have come to the kingdom for such a time as this?
(Esther 4:14).

**As William Carey said,
"Attempt great things for God.
Expect great things from God."**

*Jesus said to him, "If you can believe, all
things are possible to him who believes"*
(Mark 9:23).

Never let disappointments defeat you. God's destiny for your life is still intact. Sometimes God will allow your dreams to die in order that your destiny may live.

For I know the thoughts that I think toward you, says the Lord, thoughts of peace and not of evil, to give you a future and a hope (Jer. 29:11).

Set measurable, long-term and short-term goals. Then develop an action plan for their fulfillment.

I press toward the goal for the prize of the upward call of God in Christ Jesus (Phil. 3:14).

Only one life, 'twill soon be past.
Only what's done for Christ will last.

Live for what matters — and what matters is the exaltation of the Son of God to the ends of the earth.

And He died for all, that those who live should live no longer for themselves, but for Him who died for them and rose again (2 Cor. 5:15).

**Reputation is what you are in public.
Integrity is what you are in private.**

*Behold, You desire truth in the inward
parts, and in the hidden part You will
make me to know wisdom* (Ps. 51:6).

David Shibley *serves as president of Global Advance, a ministry training and providing resources for national church leaders to evangelize and disciple their respective nations. He is a graduate of John Brown University, Southwestern Baptist Theological Seminary, and holds an honorary doctorate from ORU. David and his wife, Naomi, have two sons, Jonathan and Joel.*

You are invited to be part of the Global Advance vision to train one million leaders to plant one million new churches worldwide. For a free copy of David's booklet, *You Can Make a World of Difference*, write or call Global Advance today.

GLOBAL ADVANCE
P.O. Box 742077
Dallas, Texas 75374-2077
(214) 771-9042
(214) 722-6119 (fax)